DODGY

FOOTBALL FASHION

Design: Glen Hind
Writing and proofing: James Cleary and Chris McLoughlin

Produced by Sport Media, Trinity Mirror North West

Executive Editor: Ken Rogers
Senior Editor: Steve Hanrahan
Senior Production Editor: Paul Dove
Senior Art Editor: Rick Cooke
Sub Editors: Roy Gilfoyle, James Cleary, Adam Oldfield
Designers: Glen Hind, Colin Sumpter, Barry Parker, Lee Ashun,
Alison Gilliland, Jamie Dunmore, James Kenyon, Lisa Critchley
Writers: Chris McLoughlin, John Hynes, Simon Hughes,
William Hughes, Alan Jewell
Sales and Marketing Manager: Elizabeth Morgan
Sales and Marketing Assistant: Karen Cadman

Published in Great Britain in 2010 by:
Trinity Mirror Sport Media,
PO Box 48, Old Hall Street, Liverpool L69 3EB.
ISBN: 9781906802400

Photographs: Mirrorpix, Trinity Mirror, PA Photos

Printed by Korotan

DODGY

FOOTBALL FASHION

Compiled by James Cleary

ALL HAIL FOOTBALL'S FASHIONABLE ROLE MODELS!

Your average star footballer may look great scoring a last-minute winner or making a vital last-ditch tackle, but what happens after the final whistle has blown and it's time to slip into something less comfortable?

Whether it's on the pull in a multi-coloured tank top, nipping down the shops in a full-length leather trench coat or simply leaning on the bonnet of their tangerine Ford Capri in a PVC suit, footballers have always had a style all their own.

The maths equation is quite simple: Young professional footballer + high disposable income = questionable fashion choices.

Like an own goal at Wembley in your only international appearance, Dodgy Football Fashion is an off-the-pitch celebration of the occasions when it has all gone so gloriously wrong.

From the 1960s – when footballers graduated from sportsmen to celebrities as easily as you might slip into a pair of velvet flares – through to the current era, there have been plenty of red-card fashion offences captured on camera. Serial offenders McCoist, Gascoigne, Keegan and Beckham seem to deserve an early bath more than most!

Dodgy Football Fashion is divided into sections but in no particular order – a bit like the walk-in wardrobe of your team's record signing. Just dive in wherever the fancy takes you.

So fair play to these spirited souls who have attempted to stand out from the crowd rather than follow the rest like sheep – which provides the perfect link to where our foul fashion odyssey kicks off: woolly jumpers, page 6.

Enjoy the book!

CONTENTS

Menacing pose

Crazy Gang, crazy clothing. Dennis Wise wears the jumper of his Beano namesake, although Dennis The Menace never embarrassed himself by wearing a Wimbledon shirt in return. Taxi for Wise... or is that a worse idea than wearing this jumper?

JUMPERS FOR GOALPOSTS

You put them down in the park for a kickaround – and some are best left there. We kick off our collection of footy fashion clangers with some woolly winter warmers that the humble fan can only dream of

Do I like orange?

Tommy Cassidy (above), brightens up Newcastle in 1971 in a jumper that's almost as bad as the Geordies' 2009/10 banana away kit

Mr and Mrs McKenzie

Duncan McKenzie should've stuck to jumping over Minis. His wife looks like she's just seen a mirror

Fancy dress?

When asked to wear their favourite jumpers, only one man, Mark Hateley, preferred his national side's leisurewear. Chris Woods (green pattern), Graham Roberts (bizarre sweatwear) and Terry Butcher (black zig-zag) show why England have never won a fashion World Cup

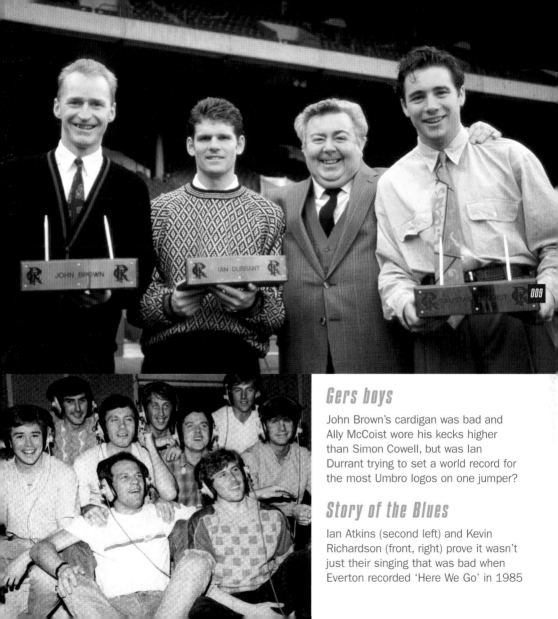

Gers boys

John Brown's cardigan was bad and Ally McCoist wore his kecks higher than Simon Cowell, but was Ian Durrant trying to set a world record for the most Umbro logos on one jumper?

Story of the Blues

Ian Atkins (second left) and Kevin Richardson (front, right) prove it wasn't just their singing that was bad when Everton recorded 'Here We Go' in 1985

Provan his best

Former Kilmarnock and Celtic star Davie Provan proves that it was acceptable to simply wear a sheep to cope with the harsh winters in Scotland in the 1980s

Boy in the bubble

If John Barnes goes shopping in a jumper that bad, imagine what must be in the bags...

Jumpers for goalies

Chelsea stopper Harry Medhurst (above) in the goalkeeping uniform of the day, March 1950

Rideout of options

Paul Rideout scored the winner in the 1995 FA Cup final a month after wearing this jumper, possibly because the Man United defence were stood around laughing

Sensible choice?

Neil Warnock celebrates his appointment as new manager of Notts County in High Street chic, although he probably blamed a referee for it...

Man of style

Ian Callaghan appears to have bought his Christmas knitwear from the same place he purchased his wallpaper in 1965

Dressed to impress?

Donny Osmond keeps an eye out for scorch marks on those 15" bell-bottoms as Oxford United players prepare for the opening of a new stand at the Manor Ground

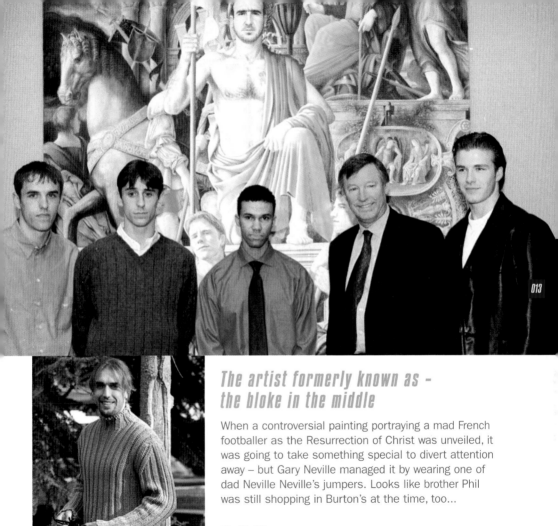

The artist formerly known as – the bloke in the middle

When a controversial painting portraying a mad French footballer as the Resurrection of Christ was unveiled, it was going to take something special to divert attention away – but Gary Neville managed it by wearing one of dad Neville Neville's jumpers. Looks like brother Phil was still shopping in Burton's at the time, too...

Bati-Woe

Gabriel Batistuta was a heart-throb to Argentinian and Italian women in the '90s. Clearly they never saw this photo

Flower power?

Gary Lineker has a hand in 'promoting' the British Clothing Industry Association. The British-made floral dress shirt with matching bow tie was available for £38. The then England captain was one of five top sports stars recruited by the BCIA to help highlight what was good about British menswear in the constant battle against fashion imports. Today, Primark goes from strength to strength…

014

LOAD OF SHIRT

**And to think that players have scrapped
to swap shirts with Lineker on the pitch...
some of these you wouldn't swap
for your nan's curtains**

015

Talent pool?

Don Revie covers up in this bathroom floor-style pattern – while the rest of the squad, including Bryan Robson (back row, second right) and Alan Curbishley (front row, right) come up short for England. Again

Hazy shirt

Man United sacked manager Tommy Docherty in 1977 for having an affair with Mary Brown, wife of club physio Laurie. They should have sacked him in 1974 for wearing a tartan blazer and signing Jim McCalliog, whose shirt inspired that blue 'bird-shit' away kit United had in 1990

Gianluigi Lentini
(or is it Peter
Andre in a wig?),
cost AC Milan
£13million in the
early 1990s.
As you can see,
he desperately
needed a move to
the fashion
capital of Europe

017

Patched up

Then Chesterfield boss John Sheridan, comfortable in a Coventry City sky blue and brown cross-stitch pattern

Peek-a-boo

John Fashanu (top left) wore black net curtains for the premiere of *Lock Stock And Two Smoking Barrels*

A man walked into a bar

George Best sports a flowery shirt which 'beautifully' off-sets the black waistcoat and tie, having attended an FA disciplinary hearing in London, September 1971, possibly for bringing fashion into disrepute

Rodeo scene

Big nose. Big cup. Big checks. A smiling cowboy-like Phil Thompson didn't pick up any fashion tips in Gay Paris when Liverpool won the European Cup there in 1981

Rhombus style

Larry Lloyd won two European Cups with Nottingham Forest. This could well be the shirt that convinced Brian Clough to wear nothing but green jumpers for 20 years

019

020

Kiss My Face!

Kevin Keegan didn't realise the table-cloth was meant to be on the table, not his back. Bet he enjoyed coming face-to-face with himself!

Roll with it

Who better to advertise the latest ball game fad – hacky sack football – than Rangers' short-sleeved Ally McCoist? Carrying a towel at all times, Brad Friedel also seems impressed in the background

Let's all have a disco

England legend Bobby Moore looks like he's turned up for a night on the town rather than a training session, unless that's a West Ham kit we've forgotten about?

How did the press spot him?

OK, it's so garish he had to wear sunglasses to look in a mirror, but this was normal attire for Gazza in the '90s, especially on trips to the dentist's (chair)

Holiday horror

That can be the only excuse for
Alan Ball's shirt, as he poses with
Arsenal team-mate Terry Mancini.
It's a classic case of A Ball
dropping A Bollock...

A maze of options

If you look close enough you can see a face in George's 'magic eye' shirt. It's fair to say it wasn't the Best

Can you spot it?

John Greig must have gone shopping with Larry Lloyd (page 19) for this number, while Kenny Dalglish wears traditional head-wear for a wee night out in Glasgae

Rough justice

Hibernian goalkeeper Alan Rough gets Bertie Auld to do his impersonation of Max from Hart to Hart. To be fair to Alan, the Pringle looks crisp

I'm a lumberjack...

He's nothing if not versatile: Davie Provan lumbers up for training

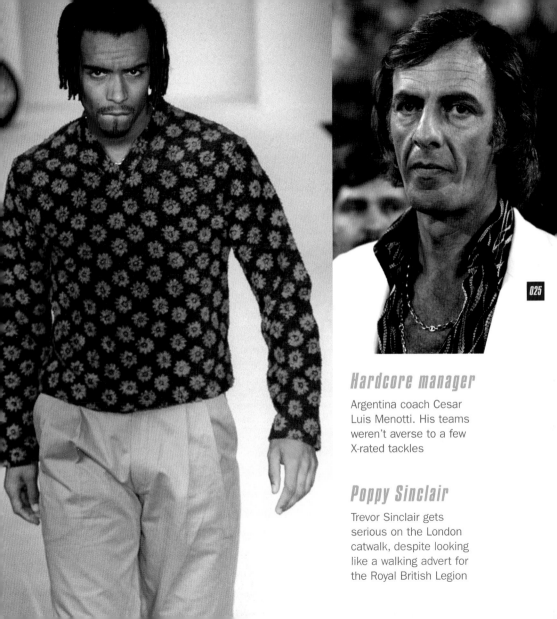

025

Hardcore manager

Argentina coach Cesar Luis Menotti. His teams weren't averse to a few X-rated tackles

Poppy Sinclair

Trevor Sinclair gets serious on the London catwalk, despite looking like a walking advert for the Royal British Legion

One size fits all

OK, so Roberto Mancini added
some Italian flair to Man City with
the scarf, but did he really need to
keep wearing it when it was so
warm that even Emmanuel
Adebayor took his gloves off?

FLIPPIN' NECK

**We wave them over our heads,
hang them out of the car window,
we even used to tie them to our wrists.
But somehow scarves only look ridiculous
when footballers decide to wear them**

027

Knot Savage

The epitome of what is wrong with the modern game, multi-millionaire Robbie portrays his own sense of style with a look straight off the pages of FHM fashion. The sharp suit, brown brogues – and, er, 'tasteful' scarf to finish. Go on. Admit it, ladies. You'd love to pull it. The scarf, that is. Obviously

Off to a tee

The Argentinian Sid James – aka 1974 World Cup coach Vladislao Cap – mixes golfing chic with eccentric neck covering

Wetting the babies' head

Champagne, cigars and natty
Fred-from-Scooby-Doo neckwear
– Neil Young (left) and Ken
Mulhearn celebrate the birth of
the former's son. Yikes!

029

Food and fashion

Dumbarton striker Ian Wallace proves that you can both eat and wear the same animal simultaneously

CARDI-GONE

Not shy of the grandfather look, our footballing heroes – be it a zip or button-up offering – are happy to utilise some additional covering to keep out the winter chill...

031

From Russia with cardigan

Zenit St Petersburg coach Yuriy Morozov could've done with an iron on his cardigan behind the iron curtain. Or a stylist

Pain in the name of style

Did Chelsea's Ian Hutchinson have to get a cardy with such a big pocket because he had hands like spades? Micky Droy bent over backwards to find bad shirts to wear

033

Saint and Cardy

Liverpool players visit Alder Hey hospital. The lads had to be careful not to get too close to the candles, in case they went up in flames

Royle knitwear

Rumours that Joe Royle wore bad cardigans because he couldn't get his big head through jumpers remain unconfirmed

Heighway to...?

Steve and his better half test the suspension of their VW Beetle and Heighway's shoes were also VW – Very Wrong. At least the former Liverpool winger had incorporated a bit of extra 'chainage' to match the Missus' lace-up boots

THE **BOOT** ROOM

Fluorescent yellow boots, flashes of red leather and pink PVC ... and that's just what they wear on the pitch these days!

Geordie driver

When Kevin Keegan sang 'Head Over Heels In Love', little did anybody know he was referring to this fetching pair of white shoes with dark heels, which were clearly popular in Newcastle. A couple of inches more and he might have reached the accelerator from there...

Fore-runner of the Predator?

Liverpool's Australian forward and future boot designer Craig Johnston shows his stuff at what can loosely be described as a 1980s fashion shoot

Tap him up

Newcastle United's Alan Kennedy felt 10-feet tall when he got to Wembley in 1974, largely because of those platforms. He'd have been better playing in them – Newcastle lost 3-0

037

I did not see it

Arsene Wenger, Arsenal manager and a man of impeccable selective eyesight, failed to glance inside his sock draw ahead of his appearance at a 2004 fashion show

039

Balls and Wilko

Everton forward Paul 'Chuckle Brother' Wilkinson displays
his unique 1980s fashion taste – the white socks being
just the tip of the iceberg. He can't even blame being
Scouse – he was born in Lincolnshire

YMcA

Benny Hill Street Blues sergeant Ally McCoist appears to be enjoying the attention. The leather police jacket and stonewash jeans could be arrestable offences in themselves – but it's the overtly camp logoed cap that wins the dodgy fashion honours here

HAT-TRICK HEROES

The only thing that should be found on some footballers' heads is a football – if some of these dubious choices in hatwear are anything to go by – on me 'ead son!

041

Head boys

Graham Moore (Chelsea) and Eddie Firmani (Charlton) opt for the classic gentleman's trilby, but Bobby Moore (West Ham) is all fur hat. Wonder if he borrowed it from a certain Russian linesman?

New York Mankees

Alf Inge Haaland will tell you Roy Keane was pretty dangerous with a football boot so imagine what he could have done with a baseball bat? Anyone fancy telling him to stick that Yankees pyjama top up his bollocks? Thought not...

Big Mack

Malcolm Allison looks more grizzly than the bear he is wearing in this picture. As for the hat – the Man from Del Monte, he say 'no'

The final straw

Midfielder Geoff Nulty in embarrassing signing headwear, 1978. Hardly the choice for Everton casuals

Italian style

Ever wondered what Tweetie Pie would look like on steroids? Alessandro del Piero reveals all. I tawt I taw a dodgy cap...

Wear it wrong

Tony Adams tries to get 'down wit da kids' by posing with Nightshade from Gladiators in a back-to-front baseball cap – but fails miserably. This is also the only known photo of Adams not appealing for offside

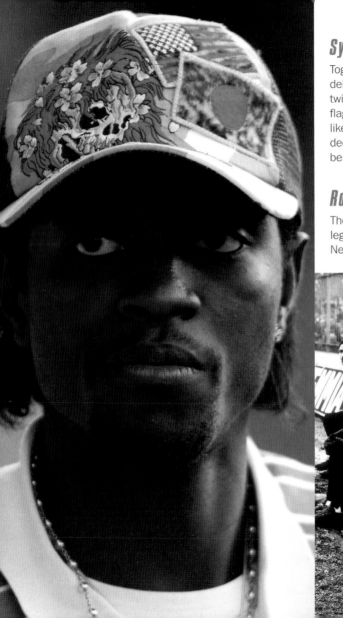

Symbol, not effective

Togo-born Emmanuel Adebayor delights in a cap showing off the twin delights of the USA and Japan flags – and what suspiciously looks like a skeleton with red hair decorated by pink flowers. Maybe it's best not to ask...

Rocco roll

The pork pie hat ensures legendary AC Milan boss Rocco Nereo stands out from the bench

045

Knight mare

Then chairman of Carlisle United, Michael Knighton was never shy of a publicity opportunity – as his failed takeover of Manchester United showed. His famous keepy-uppys in front of the Stretford End ahead of the opening game of the 1989/90 season marked him down as better than Ralph Milne, but unfortunately for Knighton, and anyone who hates United (i.e. everyone who doesn't support them), the £20m takeover deal collapsed. Instead he turned his attentions to the more sedate surrounds of Cumbria where boardroom meetings are apparently held in full football kit and bowler hat

Go Go Gadget...hat

Then at Arsenal, Robert Pires (left) attends a fancy French fashion label 'do' in London – disguised as Inspector Gadget

Tottingham Hotshares

Garth Crooks, Ossie Ardiles and Danny Thomas – the latter sans bowler hat, the spoilsport – are roped in to put on the suits and banker's hats after 'Tottingham' were floated on the London Stock Exchange in 1983. That's BANKER'S hats...

047

FINANCIAL TIMES

Shameless plugs

Nottingham Forest's Nigel Clough and Stuart Pearce try to set a new record for plugging the most things in one photo when they hail the triple merits of water consumption, telecommunications and Shredded Wheat. Who forgot the milk?

On the flip side...

Here's another Forest player in the form of Terry Wilson, sporting shades and a Joe Bloggs number 'of its time' in 1991

049

And there's more

You'll never beat Des Walker and you'll never look as stupid as Steve Chettle did when he tried to wear a Volvic baseball cap above his head – instead of on it

050

Mr Crisp

Gary Lineker, as the face of
Walkers Crisps, has appeared
in a series of campaigns
which have required him to
dress in outfits of varying
degrees of embarrassment,
including a Leicester City
shirt. And, yes, the cap studs
spell out W.A.L.K.E.R.S.

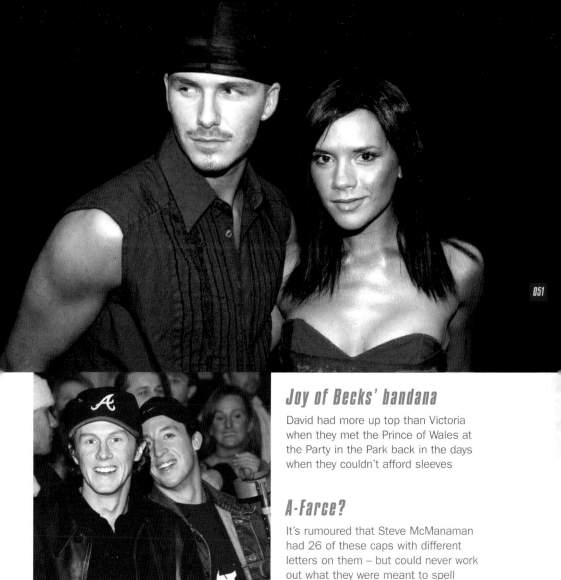

051

Joy of Becks' bandana

David had more up top than Victoria when they met the Prince of Wales at the Party in the Park back in the days when they couldn't afford sleeves

A-Farce?

It's rumoured that Steve McManaman had 26 of these caps with different letters on them – but could never work out what they were meant to spell

Nutty boys

Barry Venison and Gary Pallister get the baseball gear out, including oversized sponsors' hats, because England were playing the USA. Just to clarify, England were playing them at football so what that had to do with Barry and Pally is unclear

Tea cosy

Juventus goalkeeper Gianluigi Buffon (below) looks more like a buffoon in this woolly hat. He must have one cold tea-pot at home

052

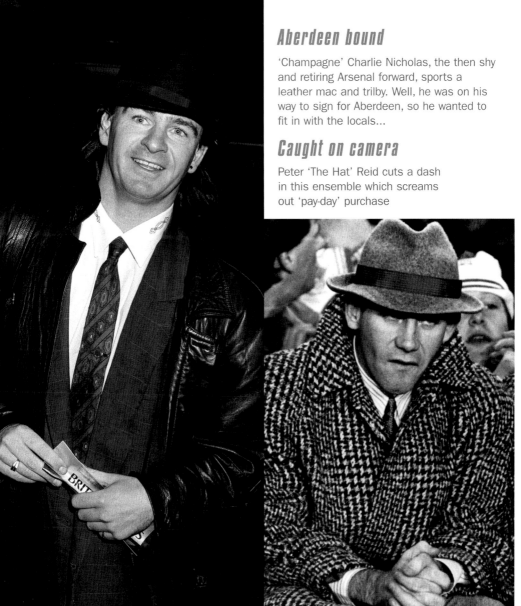

Aberdeen bound

'Champagne' Charlie Nicholas, the then shy
and retiring Arsenal forward, sports a
leather mac and trilby. Well, he was on his
way to sign for Aberdeen, so he wanted to
fit in with the locals...

Caught on camera

Peter 'The Hat' Reid cuts a dash
in this ensemble which screams
out 'pay-day' purchase

053

You lookin' at me?

Oh God, what's my
father wearing?
Becks goes for the
Robert De Niro look
on the school run

055

Any old Iron

Cricket legend Ian Botham also turned out for Scunthorpe during his sporting days. He was often not out for England, and he should not have been out in that trilby

The power of advertising

Portuguese midfielder Manuel Fernandes, looking like a cross between an extra from *Fame* – and a walking advert for an American lager

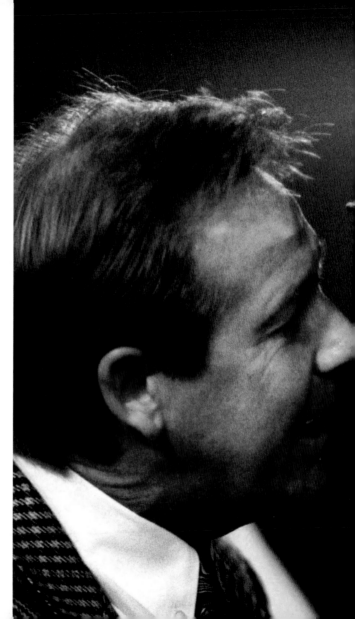

Worthy Cowboy

Leicester City PA announcer and
former star Alan Birchenall MBE
interviews ex-team-mate Frank
Worthington on the pitch. Alan's
jacket could perhaps be worthy
of his own page, but sadly for
Frank it was Paul Hogan who got
to play Crocodile Dundee.
You call that a hat? This is a hat

Red carpet mode

Vinnie Jones turned up at the premiere of *Mean Machine* sporting a pork pie trilby and a white ferret. Oh, you're not ferret good...

Top hat!

Top Hat! The ineffectual, Top Hat! Looks intellectual, close friends get to call him MO, but then you'll see his hamstrings go...

The Watford Cap

Sir Elton John's hat is so big
it could probably bridge the
North-South divide

Sign for Bhoys

Gianluca Vialli checks to see nobody
else is wearing a cap as stylish as his
while simultaneously signing anything
put in front of him. He adopted a
similar transfer policy as Chelsea boss

059

060

Man of style

Arsenal's Charlie Nicholas,
which is how a lot of
women he met ended up,
revels in the pop star look

IN THE SHADE

**The ultimate rock star accessory,
the epitome of 'cool', it wasn't long
before trendy eyewear was taken on by the
footballing classes – some of these are more
three-match bans than Raybans though**

Smooth opewator

Manager Woy Hodgson (above) bwings the wock 'n' woll style to a gwound near you

Bloody Tourists

It's a funny old look. Jimmy Greaves tries these shades on for size (left) ahead of the 1962 World Cup finals in Chile. England played worse than Greavsie looks

Poor sods

One man went to mow... then realised there was no grass. Check the tablecloth shirt and tweed hat combo, complete with stylish sunglasses, as worn by then Chelsea boss Eddie McCreadie, February 1977

England's finest

(Above, left to right) Kevin Keegan, Gerry Francis and Mick Channon relax in different shades at Heathrow Airport. They were flying to Glasgow, making the sunglasses about as much use as alcohol-free lager up there

Looks the type

Neil Warnock wears sunglasses while manager of Bury. They say he changes when the sun goes down...

Soft rock

Former USA international defender Alexei Lalas retains the unkempt look of his Serie A footballing heyday – complete with 'cool' shades

Duncan had some sunglasses

Forced to don regulation Everton team tracksuit, Duncan Ferguson was determined to make himself stand out from the crowd – or more likely hide a black eye from whoever he'd had his latest scrap with

Sign of the times

Scottish midfielder Simon Donnelly had a lot of injury problems during his time at Sheffield Wednesday. This may or may not have been down to his penchant for pretending to surf dressed like a member of East 17 in the most unusual places, such as, er, Sheffield. The top is Tommy Hilfiger, the shades were two-for-£10 on Sheffield Market

066

Italian's dream

Gabriel Batistuta attempts to blend in with Fiorentina fans after arriving at Barcelona Airport. The bright purple tracksuit may have given him away, but this didn't bother Thelma from Scooby Doo

Glass-eyed boys

Eye coverage again fails to mask the outfits on offer as the England squad try on their new glasses, April 1975. Left to right, top: Fred Street (physio), Alan Ball, Alan Hudson, Dave Watson, Colin Todd. Left to right, front: Kevin Beattie, Dennis Tueart, Colin Bell, Emlyn Hughes and Roger Kenyon

Some glasses

Where on earth did Sam Allardyce find a pair of shades that fit his head?

069

A shade unlucky

Good job Shilts wasn't wearing these specs in the World Cup of 1986 – they might have been knocked off by a flying Hand of God. Clem must've had these on when he let that Kenny Dalglish shot slip through his legs at Wembley in '77

Shades of God

Speaking of Mexico '86 ... here's Maradona in dark glasses more suited to wacky funster Timmy Mallett (or a lady)

Dangerous colouring from Bruce Grobbelaar as he arrives for an underwhelming appearance at Winchester Crown Court in the 1990s. He must have been nervous – but at least the mac covered up his spaghetti legs

070

MAC AND ME

Popularised in recent years courtesy of BBC throwback show *Life On Mars*, the 'flasher's mac' has been in and out of fashion with footballers and sheepskin-snubbing managers through the years...

071

072

Danish bacon

A spell in charge of FC Copenhagen clearly had an impact on Roy Hodgson's all-weather wear, and he discovered he could bend his thumb like a pig's willy

Older Bhoy

Charlie Nicholas in Simple Minds mode – like the panel on Sky's Soccer Saturday then...

Return of die Mack

Franz Beckenbauer and Ottmar Hitzfeld seem somewhat concerned that the European Cup has turned up without a coat on

Earning their Spurs

Tottenham officials cover up for an FA Commission Inquiry

Do you want my autograph?

Ossie Ardiles gets the autograph of new Arsenal sensation Peter Marinello in 1970, before crossing the road to sign for Spurs

Return of the Mac

Tommy Gemmell (right) keeps it closed

Harry's game

Harry Redknapp wheels-and-deals in the transfer market like an East End wide-boy – and dresses like one too. Must've got that mac from a mush in Shepherd's Bush

Gone Dutch

Guus Hiddink used to have two chins, one massive moustache, one giant cup and the shortest-sleeved mac in Europe during his PSV Eindhoven days

Dodgy tone

Tony Yeboah makes an eye-catching impression as he meets Hamburg coach Bernd Wehmeyer while perfecting the chessboard-on-acid look we all strive for

NO JACKET REQUIRED

When Shoot magazine asked footballers who their favourite musician was during the eighties, Phil Collins was probably the top answer, closely followed by Level 42's bass-slapping Mark King. Naff choices? See what you make of these...

Yellow peril

Johan should've done a Cruyff turn back into his house and put something fashionable on as soon as he saw the camera. Hi-de-Hi!

Private property

Kevin Keegan needs to work on perfecting the country squire look before he visits the Woolsington Hall home of Sir John Hall again

Kick it out

The day after the night before, a colourful Eric Cantona leaves home having kung-fu kicked a Crystal Palace supporter the previous night. Comedy legend Benny Hill turned up to give him some moral support. Pity he forgot his glasses – could have saved the pair of them from another vulgar display in public

Searching for a new jacket

What better way to spot seagulls following the trawler than to disguise yourself as a deckchair?

Shorts sighted

There must have been a fog on the Tyne when Gazza got ready. He was apparently helping to publicise a TV documentary 'Gazza: The Fight Back' and his attire suggests there was quite a long way to go...

Straight out of Top Man

Natty woolly mac, trendy trilby – Peter Reid looks like he's off to sell watches

Pish and Becks

Where's the zip again Victoria? Becks and Missus hold it all in – not an outfit you'd recommend if you get caught short

081

Patchwork offering

George Best could afford expensive wheels, but apparently not to replace his old patched-up jacket

Night on the bathroom tiles

George's jacket appears to have been designed by the makers of Tetris, or bathroom flooring, as he chats to his mentor Sir Matt Busby – with Benny Hill laughing in the background

Frank style

Frank Lampard was doing a shift in
the ice-cream parlour after launching
his new book to the world's press

Instant Karma?

A working-class hero is something
to be, but that doesn't excuse
Celtic's Neil Lennon (top left) from
looking for a kick-off in an art
gallery wearing an inside-out leather

Big shoulders

West Germany boss Sepp Herberger
(left) wraps up as he speaks to
Horst Szymaniak during a training
session at Berlin's Olympic Stadium

084

Multi-coloured coat and mullet

Just in case anyone thought a multi-coloured shell-suit jacket went well with jeans and brown shoes, Davie Provan proves not

Full yellow jacket

Bulgaria legend Hristro Stoichkov cut the 'mustard' for Barcelona, but could do with cutting out the mustard jacket. It clashes with his tan

Zip it up

The dodgy jacket could at least mask the stripey shirt on Alan Hudson, who had just signed for Chelsea for a then British record £240,000. Money well spent? Not on the clothes

Man in corduroy coat on a football pitch

The man, the legend –
in fact, it's actually
mid-1960s Aston Villa
boss Dick Taylor

Got any claret?

Teddy boy David Sullivan
celebrates his successful
purchase of half of West Ham
by dressing like a 1980s
cinema usher

086

Bad smell

At least Hearts' Gary MacKay
dressed as a chef for this snap. If the
onion John Robertson is cutting didn't
make him cry, the jacket should have

Pat, got any The The?

He isn't Smashy and there's
nothing Nicey about Pat Nevin's
leather jacket

Exciting times

Ally McCoist's jacket masks
him from the nip in the air...

Rodney you plonker

Rodney Marsh – complete with figure-hugging slacks – after signing for Manchester City. At least his mouth is shut, for a change

087

Is he worth it?

Presumably Ashley Cole didn't text any pictures of himself in this jacket to other women before escorting his X Mrs to X Factor auditions

Latest fashion

Paul Gascoigne models what was officially dubbed as 'young man about town' clobber in his Newcastle days. It's not the last time he's been pictured propping up a bar

Thumbs up for Macs

Thank goodness Kevin Keegan had his kecks on when he wore this 'flasher' mac-style effort during his Hamburg days

Baggy boy

Ryan Giggs tries to think of a time when denim jackets were considered fashionable...

All in the presentation

Gary Lineker gladly accepted a trophy for best impression of a walking Everton mint

Long arm of the jacket

Gianfranco Zola wears a jacket that is plainly too big for him, a problem he's had ever since he stopped shopping at Mothercare

Patched up

Paul Gascoigne was unable to play the bagpipes, so dressed like a set of them instead

Shine a light

Despite his best attempts, John Barnes was beaten by Jim Carrey to the lead role in *The Mask*

A white liberty

No need to send for the men in white coats with Rio Ferdinand about. He even remembered to turn up in it...

091

Well red

This figure-hugging long-sleeved polo top saw Celtic's Murdo MacLeod become the inspiration behind the characters in Cluedo. Even Roy Baines and perennial fashion victim Davie Provan knew he looked daft

POLO NOT SO MINT

**Polo is an upper-class sport.
That's the way it should remain if these
jumpers sported by football's working class
heroes are anything to go by**

Tartan overkill

Larry Lloyd always wore
a white polo-neck and
jacket when sitting
behind a wooden fence

Feeling blue

Alan Hudson and Peter
Osgood contribute to the
recording of 'Blue is the
Colour' by proving that
fashion isn't their game.
Peter's voice was a bit hoarse
that day, which might explain
the saddlebags around
his neck

Big 'ead,
big polo-neck

"I wouldn't say I was the best manager in the business, but I was in the top one." We wouldn't say that was the worst polo-neck/jacket combination in the business, but...

One stripe

When Bobby Moore's brown suede jacket was made there was a bit of material left over so he wore it around his neck

Gorgeous George

George Graham
shows off some
'boring, boring'
high-neck knitwear

Eusebio style

Would Cristiano Ronaldo
wear a woolly polo-neck? No,
and that's why Eusebio
remains the great man of
Portuguese football. Gordon
Banks congratulates him on
his obvious style

Polo boy

News just in. Woolly polo-neck jumpers don't suit Peter Shilton

097

City not on song

Manchester City players prepare to board the train ahead of the FA Cup final against Leicester City dressed like a male voice choir. Left to right: Alan Oakes, Mike Doyle, Colin Bell, Neil Young and Tony Coleman

Dig for victory

Kevin Keegan was always
good at staying on his feet.
Only problem today is he can't
find them anywhere

RIGHT OLD FLARE UP

**Foreign fans love setting flares on fire.
These boys should have done the same**

Beginning of the end?

'Shoot us now in case we embarrass ourselves against Zaire.' Danny McGrain and Jim Stewart weigh up the odds with the West German police academy before the Scots embark on the 1974 World Cup campaign

Balls up

...is what Tony Mowbray made of Celtic, unlike... Danny McGrain, Kenny Dalglish, Harry Hood and Tom Callaghan – proving that you can have flair in flares

Stroll in the park

Everton players keep off the grass to avoid muddy flares in 1977

A flare for invention

Far left: Charlie George, superstar, is forced to lap the training ground with his hands stuck in his velvet blazer. The idea was to prevent him lying on the turf and throwing his arms in the air in annoying celebratory fashion

To be Frank...

"Your jeans are too tight, son!"
What Bob Paisley might have said to Mr Worthington (left) after failing his medical at Liverpool, June 1972

Mickey Mouse stuff

Somebody should have told
Kevin Keegan his nickname at
Liverpool was MIGHTY Mouse...
still, there's plenty to take the
Mickey out of here

102

Put a crease in it

Graeme Souness
dresses appropriately
for a night out in
Middlesbrough. They
still dress like that on
Teesside now...

103

21st century boy

Jesus... this trend-heavy T-shirt was the most memorable part of Karl Svensson's Rangers career

YOU'RE (CASUAL) SHIRT, AAAARGH!

From home shirts to put them away ones

Top pocket

Liverpool's Tony Hateley goes for the top pocket that doesn't have a packet of fags already in it

What a sparkler

Goalkeeper Carlo Nash shows what can happen if you let the kids loose with glitter in your wardrobe

Summer boys

Paul Gascoigne and Paul Stewart (understated logo) are welcomed to Tottenham Hotspur by boss Terry Venables – but if your initials were 'TV' would you really want to broadcast it?

Tim nice but not so Dim

Tim Cahill deserves to be punched by a corner flag for wearing this casual T-shirt

Salad days

Neil Warnock again. Involved in another bun fight at Notts County

Purple haze

Scotland's finest Davie Provan raises the stakes in a more feminine hue as he poses with girlfriend Fiona, November 1986

Sven will I see you again?

A youthful Sven-Goran Eriksson sits on his ball, waiting for the women to queue up

Leg it

Tight shirt and baggy 'kecks' combo – West Ham skipper Billy Bonds used to race against his pet greyhound 'Toby' to get fit. The dog was quicker, and better dressed

Lilian Savage

France defender Lilian Thuram with a
T-shirt to almost tie-dye for...

More skull than skill

El-Hadji Diouf has worn that much dodgy
clobber that we could fill the entire book with
it, but this was special. Apparently, the
diamond-encrusted skull on his belt cost
thousands. It's probably not the only skeleton
Diouf has in his closet

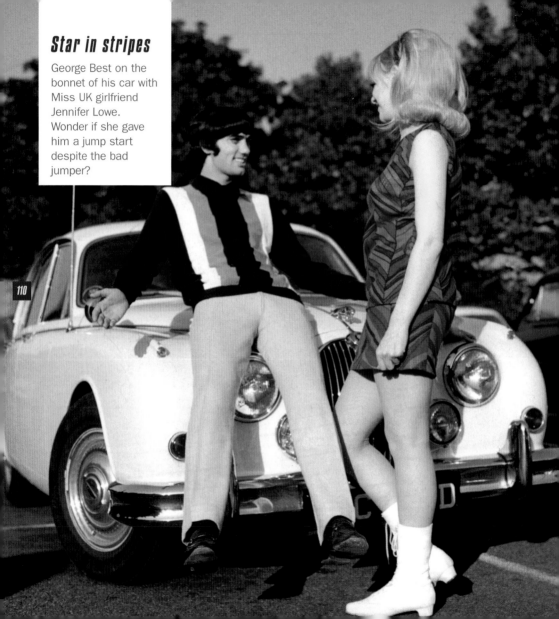

Star in stripes

George Best on the bonnet of his car with Miss UK girlfriend Jennifer Lowe. Wonder if she gave him a jump start despite the bad jumper?

110

STARS IN STRIPES

Fans of Stoke City, Newcastle United and West Brom among others will know about the feelgood factor of wearing stripes around town. However, there isn't much that feels good about some of these...

I don't care how good you are...

Pele reveals the number of people who admitted they would be seen dead in such a bad suit

Ice to see you

Eric Cantona shows off the most fashionable attire that an ice-cream man could ever hope to wear to work

Man of hoops

Kevin Keegan would love it if you took a photo of him dressed like Dennis The Menace, love it

113

Blues stripe

Chelsea players look classy as ever on Bournemouth beach. One of them gets away with 'plain' shorts – was he the original special one?

Bo Jangles

There's certainly nothing wrong with Trevor Francis's retro T-shirt and 'T' cup – but surely it's flamboyant starlet Keith Bertschin catching the eye, dripping in gold, as the pair sport his and his plaster casts in 1978

True love

Marina Dalglish still loved husband Kenny even though he insisted on mixing big brown patterned collars with woolly stripes

Oh Stripes

The dangers of collared, striped shirts – as worn by Coventry City managing director Jimmy Hill and manager Gordon Milne. Even the balls at Coventry wore stripes

Man in wool

Unfortunately, Everton legend Mick Lyons washed his hair and jumper at the wrong temperature and it all got a bit fluffy

French connection

Tight 'leather' opened to show off a jumper which wouldn't look out of place on the streets of Paris. Leicester City's Alan Birchenall and Keith Weller 'pose as Brett Sinclair and his side-kick Danny out of The Persuaders'. They should have been persuaded to get changed

116

It could be Cole

Ashley remembers a time when all this white suit-wearing posing with a publicity-shy better half would have been deemed mere farce

SUITS YOU, SIR

The tradition of the cup final suits, a memorable moment in the career of a footballer. Unfortunately, such was the fuss created by Liverpool's 1996 white Armani suits that ever since, there has been a proliferation of dull fare on offer. That has not stopped the odd smattering of daring from some who should know better – while there's also a nod to earlier times...

117

The sacrifices England players have to make

You know it's a bad suit when even Kevin Keegan thinks it looks ridiculous. Peter Shilton seems happier with the dapper design, while Mick Channon and Alan Ball wisely stick to their 'civvies'

Breit velvet

Paul Breitner's hair – and suit – surely designed with X-rated movies in mind. Robbie Savage's German uncle sports a decent kipper tie, too

Red or dread?

He didn't stand out on the pitch so Kevin Harper ensures he did off it. Kenny Miller and Kris Boyd look expensively dull in comparison

Pack it in

Frank Worthington (left, right in picture) performing with the Grumbleweeds. A big Elvis Presley fan, Frank was happy to sing, dance and dress in the style of his hero...although no-one ever dressed in the style of Frank

Monstrous monster

Football agent and one-time media
personality Eric Hall arrives at an
envelope-opening awards bash

Trendy feather

Fabrizio Ravanelli shines on the
catwalk in Milan, sporting a designer-
on-acid creation that he may have
bought in Middlesbrough

Reds and white Armani

Steve Bruce spots that John Barnes and Liverpool think they've come to London for a day out boating on the Thames, rather than to play in the FA Cup final

Them Scousers again

At least Robbie Fowler takes the white suits in good heart, as Jamie Redknapp tries, but fails, to look cool in shades

Suited and booted?

Nottingham Forest manager Brian Clough realised his suit was so bad that he tried to walk through as many puddles as possible to cover it in mud

Baggy Ally

Ally McCoist had enough room to eat deep-fried Mars bars every day – and still get into his suit

Creased Up

Beige seems to be the colour for Bolton Wanderers boss Sam Allardyce – while his assistant, pre-stylish scarf phase Phil Brown, proves that it wasn't just sunny in Hull

123

Natural body (language)

Kevin Keegan again proves he's a natural for the camera – be thankful he's not wearing the hotpants and jumper

Gerry and Terry

The ideal photo op: a dodgy pitch, stripy pants, Gerry Francis and Terry Venables helping out the QPR groundsman. It is around this point that El Tel may have dreamt up a Loftus Road future with a plastic pitch

Brown-suited boy

Did anyone actually buy a suit that Davie Provan modelled? Hopefully not

The original red

Newcastle manager Kevin Keegan hails the signing of Les Ferdinand by dressing up as Richard Keys

125

Money can't buy you class

With matching splash-design sky blue and black jacket plus dickie bow, Franz Beckenbauer is hard to miss. It's unknown whether first wife Brigitte cited the jacket as a reason for their divorce

126

Best dressed?

David Beckham – then named as one of the world's best-dressed men by US magazine Vanity Fair. The magazine is still trying to restore its credibility

One may not have been amused

John Barnes went to Buckingham Palace to receive his MBE from the Queen dressed like this. Honestly

Green man

Barcelona's Johan Cruyff tries to convince Real Madrid manager Benito Floro (far right) that he got the green jacket after winning The Masters

Sunday best

Liverpool players including Kevin Keegan and Phil Thompson celebrate a trophy-laden season in fancy dress. At least, that should have been their excuse for such horrendous clobber

Paddy takes the Mick

It suddenly dawns on Mick Martin (right) that the only thing worse than his awful suit and tie combination is meeting Paddy Crerand in an equally bad tie

Man about town

West Ham's Geoff Hurst looks straight ahead and pretends he isn't with Arsenal's Bob McNab and the twonk in the tank top, Peter Marinello. They were due to model at a charity showing of Playboy international menswear collection – can't think why they chose that gig...

TANKS, BUT NO TANKS

A 1970s fashion staple, it appears footballers have always been fond of a piece of extra material. Perhaps it was snooker legend John Virgo's fault, the *Big Break* 'maestro' who'd don a different waistcoat before reeling off an awful gag on the 1990s BBC show. Mind you, it did at least provide some respite from comedian Jim Davidson's 'unique' brand of patter...

Follow the boss

Paul Mariner (right) attempts to replicate his former Ipswich Town boss Bobby Robson's woollen wear alongside Bryan Robson on England duty

Sharp shooter

Everton's Graeme Sharp in baize action

He's tanked

How could a woollen affair ever complement that shirt? Evidently Sunderland's Bobby Kerr didn't care that he looked ridiculous

Give me that back

Kevin Keegan gives some style advice to a fellow V-neck wool wearer, Newcastle schoolboy Ian Bogie. Unfortunately it seems like he listened to him

Sack the stylist

Manager Bill Shankly struggles to mask his disapproval of Kevin Keegan's tank top after the latter signed for Liverpool. Shankly is probably the only bloke who could have got away with wearing a pink shirt in front of the Kop at Anfield

Scots guard

Tartan-tied Colin Hendry may not have been so keen to sign for Coventry City if he had known about Gordon Strachan's waistcoat. Or his tactics. Or the world-famous South American striker he had lined up...

Peru the hell are you?

Gordon Strachan welcomes another new addition to Coventry in similar attire – Peruvian suit Ysrael Zuniga. No, us neither

133

Tanks a lot

Frank Lampard Junior is built like a tank and Frank Lampard Senior used to wear tank tops. Note the way he offsets the stripes with those on his tea cup. If only West Ham had been so co-ordinated on the pitch

Virgin on the fashionable?

Arsenal legend Tony Adams plays it safe by opting for stripes everywhere

100-500

Tyneside style

A mulletted Chris
Waddle takes in his
new surroundings
after joining
Tottenham Hotspur.
The hair was bad,
the jacket worse

TARTAN TERRORS

The tartan influence is a fashion trend that footballers – whether Scottish or otherwise – have been only too happy to take on board down the years...

135

Man of the people

Vinnie Jones keeping it real as he enjoys the horse racing spectacle at Royal Ascot dressed like a Burberry fashion victim

Is it a funny old shot?

Top left: We can understand Tommy Docherty (centre) and Ian St John (right) being decked out in tartan, but Jimmy Greaves?

Tartan tinge

Coventry City's Neil Martin tartans himself up alongside Ernie Hunt, boxer Peter Boddington and George Curtis to push over pennies for charity. He could have done with spending a few on a new jacket

Chop Souey's adviser

Graeme Souness making the ultimate fashion statement in polo neck, flared trousers and tartan coat. Hadn't he noticed the shop sold decent gear too?

Imre joins the Bay City Rollers

Everton's new signing Imre Varadi (below) gurns like it's 1975, in, erm, 1979

Legend (in his own household) meets Pele

Then Scotland boss Andy Roxburgh outfoxes the Brazilian legend in this offering straight from the back of the wardrobe, which is where it should have stayed

Old wotshisname

Jack Charlton blends coat with tartan trousers while manager of Middlesbrough. He was too well dressed at the time to get the Ireland job

A right kilt

We can confirm that no animals were hurt during the making of this book. Mo Johnston probably can't say the same about his outfit

Don with this sort of thing

Leeds' legendary manager Don Revie in one Ell of a bad jacket

Mister, can I have your autograph?

Everton manager Harry Catterick dons the traditional tartan jacket wear for the coach journey with his squad. Despite this, some kid still wanted his autograph

Dirty McLeeds

United's Scottish contingent gets kilted out. Back row left to right: Joe Jordan, Asa Hartford, Gordon McQueen. Front left to right: Eddie Gray, Peter Lorimer, Billy Bremner, Frank Gray. Dodgy clobber and they knew all about clobbering people

The stuff of legend

Give praise indeed to King Kev's tartan lining, as he relaxes at the team hotel with fellow badly dressed England squad members (left to right) David Johnson, Phil Thompson and Mick Channon

Sporting casual

Peter Shilton presumably had a round of golf booked after training… although we're not sure if his admirers were invited. The England goalkeeper, Stoke City manager Tony Waddington's record signing, was reporting to the Victoria Ground for the first time as a Potters player. The first to greet him were some of the Stoke "MUMS", the ladies who apparently boarded the club's junior players – and quite possibly dressed Shilton, too

Leading by example

Manchester United manager Tommy Docherty and George Best were both on the lookout for a stylist

A million pounds

Tartan-clad 'Big' Malcolm Allison welcomes Norwich City's Kevin Reeves to Maine Road in traditional Mancunian attire

Sam and Dons

Not only has Vinnie Jones's acting career gone to his head, his clothes have gone to plaid. Samantha Janus and John Fashanu try to look like they're laughing WITH him...

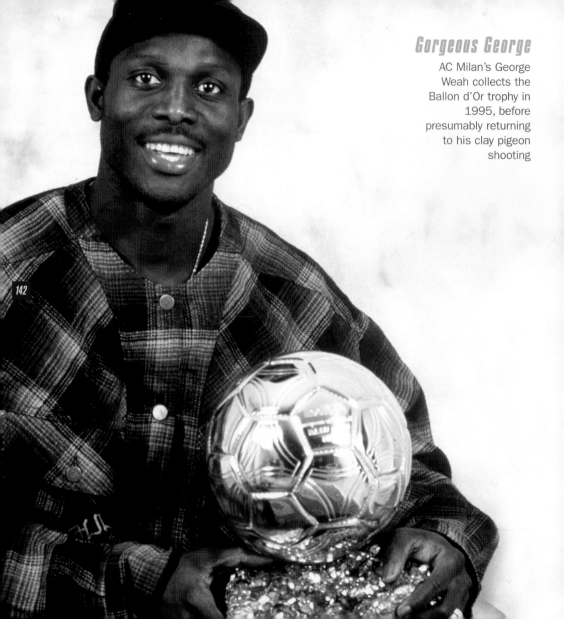

Gorgeous George

AC Milan's George Weah collects the Ballon d'Or trophy in 1995, before presumably returning to his clay pigeon shooting

THE TWEEDY

The old-fashioned country gent fashions on display – as worn by the great and good of the football world...

143

144

Milan fashion

Italy and AC legend Gianni Rivera in tartan tweed. Aren't the Italians meant to be fashionable? Should have gone to Rivera Island

Tartan tweed

Bobby Collins (left) and other Leeds team-mates including Billy Bremner and Jack Charlton borrowed their jackets off local Yorkshire farmers

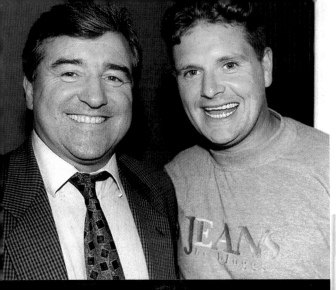

Wear It Tel

Terry Venables was no Fabio Capello when it came to fashion, and Gazza's T-shirt reminds him what to wear on his legs

Model Mellor

Burnley goalkeeper Peter Mellor wears the fox hunter look well. They apparently still catch dinner in Burnley like that nowadays

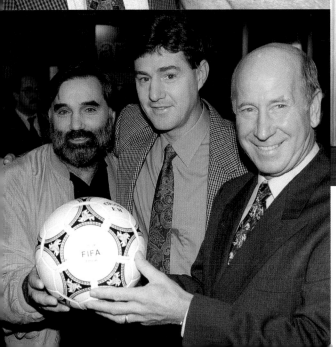

In The Kidd Of It

Brian Kidd opts for hint of Burberry, Bobby Charlton a traditional suit and George Best wears whatever he woke up in. Even so, it's better than Kiddo's jacket

Simply the Vest
Charlie Nicholas and then girlfriend Suzanne Dando. No further comment is needed

THE VERY VEST

The humble vest, traditionally worn by athletes and people keen to keep the cold out. These sporting stars aren't shy to show off their lightweight garments – if anyone's going to look good in one, then surely it'll be the cream of the football world...

The vest a man can get

Where did it go wrong for George?!? Best celebrates his 26th birthday in Marbella – where he announced his 'retirement' from football and from wearing anything remotely fashionable

So Marcel

Desailly could've done with investing in some better clothes

Sparky Moment

Anyone who still questions Mark Hughes's sacking as Man City manager should bear this photo in mind. Perhaps Sheikh Mansour did

149

Furry bad

Sol Campbell considers the value of his image rights. Our guess is £0

150

THEY'RE A BIT SHEEPISH

Imagining John Motson without a sheepskin is a bit like picturing Dickie Davies without that lick of white paint in his hair... but he's not the only one who's tried to pull the wool over our eyes down the years.
Fur play to them...

151

Two pics only?

Craig Johnston makes the kind of gesture he should have given to John Motson when he sold him his sheepskin coat

Super Furry Allison

The coat's a bit special on Malcolm Allison (above), as he salutes the crowd following his return to Manchester City. Anyone for a Big Mac and Fleas?

Sunday Driver

The sheepskin coat, the leather gloves – Walton & Hersham (and future Wimbledon) manager Allen Batsford looks prepared for Sunday driving in 1973

You can't win them all

Sheepskin-clad Don Revie and trainer Les Cocker look as cold as each other despite one being in a tracksuit and the other wearing a bear

Phil Brown's Phil Brown Jacket

The sunbed-shy ex-Hull City manager attracts the housewives' attention with this collar. At least he wasn't singing

153

Sheepish

That coat – anything to take attention away from Bob McNab's tie – as he attends an FA Disciplinary Committee at Lancaster Gate

Just one cornetto. Give it to her

Italian playmaker Antonio Cassano (above right) makes an impact upon signing for Real Madrid in half a fox. His inglorious on-field spell with the club contrasted sharply with his prodigious appetite for ladies. In his 2008 book 'Vi Dico Tutto' (I'll Tell You Everything), he revealed of his prowess with the opposite sex during his time in Spain: 'In Madrid it was easier, because we were in a hotel, the whole squad and staff on one floor, so on the floors above or below you could invite whoever you wanted to meet you during the night. I made friends with one of the waiters. His job was to bring me 3 or 4 cornetti (pastries not ice-creams!) after I had sex. He would bring the cornetti to the stairs, I would bring the girl and we would make a trade: he took the girl, I stuffed myself with cornetti. Sex plus food, the perfect night'

A crisp jacket

Prodigal son Gary Lineker, then at Barcelona, meets young Leicester City fans on a visit back to his first club

On a (Eastern European) promise

Leeds United players Johnny Giles and Mick Jones arrive at Manchester Victoria station, on their way to Ringway Airport. Their coats were put in quarantine shortly afterwards

Gazza and Digger

When England fans hoped for Paul Gascoigne and John Barnes to be involved in a thrilling World Cup tie, this wasn't what they had in mind

TIE ME UP

They've all been involved in embarrassing cup ties down the years and have rightfully earned a place in our Knotts County reserves squad

Through the blue haze

Ron Atkinson may have just realised that Forest are live on TV – and his tie is from a charity shop

Davie keeps quiet

Clothes horse Provan (above middle), now in his media guise and fellow talking head Jim White (above left), can only admire the leather-clad, bad tie, earring-wearing Mark Hateley for dressing like that in a public place

Stupid Gurn

Ally McCoist, with Gers' team-mate Ian Ferguson, in a Rangers club suit

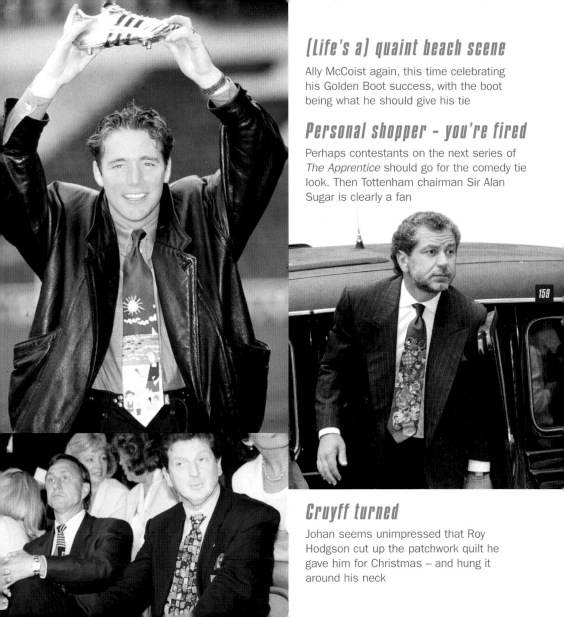

(Life's a) quaint beach scene

Ally McCoist again, this time celebrating his Golden Boot success, with the boot being what he should give his tie

Personal shopper - you're fired

Perhaps contestants on the next series of *The Apprentice* should go for the comedy tie look. Then Tottenham chairman Sir Alan Sugar is clearly a fan

Cruyff turned

Johan seems unimpressed that Roy Hodgson cut up the patchwork quilt he gave him for Christmas – and hung it around his neck

A big heart these days

Dion Dublin's heart-based psychedelia overwhelms the tartan-tinged jacket of then Man United team-mate Darren Ferguson who considers Dion's advice about growing a bumfluff tache so he looks old enough to get past the Hacienda bouncers

Gone down like the...

A smartly-attired Gianluca Vialli (below left) is overshadowed by Roberto Di Matteo's 'sick tie' at the premiere of *Titanic*. Di Matteo had gone overboard, appropriately

160

Polka-dot tinge

Ally McCoist could do with a visit from Trinny and Susannah. Rangers team-mate Pieter Huistra is next in the queue for advice

A load of old (no) shirt

Here are two pictures of Freddie Ljungberg collecting his Swedish Player of the Year award in an unnecessarily open shirt and a belting tie. If you saw a mate dressed like that, you'd belt him

162

Bobby in his shell

Having just won the FA Cup, Roberto Di Matteo must have realised people would spot him dressed like this – but still he went out

TRACKSUIT MANAGER

Sporting leisurewear made apparently famous by male north-west residents sporting tashes and big frizzy hair, the original style icons of the football world made their mark well before a 1990s comedy sketch show popularised 'comfort' wear...

Red men

Aberdeen manager Alex Ferguson spat his chewing gum out for this photoshoot. Unfortunately it landed on Gordon Strachan's sensible jumper and the pair were inseparable

Snodin Times

Ian Snodin signed for Everton in a Puma tracksuit, possibly to try and fit in with the fans

Travelling in comfort

Manager Howard Kendall and his Everton players (left to right) Adrian Heath, Andy Gray and Peter Reid looked far from atrack-tive boarding this flight

What a Joker!

Chris Waddle poses for a picture with Batman, and it was a Dark (K)night for England when he missed in the penalty shoot-out against West Germany at the 1990 World Cup

Wor Bobby

Ipswich Town boss Bobby Robson – when tracksuits didn't need a logo, July 1971

Fila good?

Wrexham's Mickey Thomas appears in court on a charge of distributing counterfeit currency. A counterfeit tracksuit couldn't have been worse

What a Le Coq

Neil Warnock hails himself for
wearing the worst tracksuit
seen in football in the 1980s

Fit for Gladiators

'Fash the Bash' may well
have been flash with cash
for doing this Hummel
leisurewear shoot with
model 'Twizzle Forster' (yes,
really). It's believed he
practised by leaping over
Dennis Wise in training

'Ignore her, she's nuts...'

Bobby Moore greets Brazilian legend
Carlos Alberto at Upton Park. The
Brazilian's actress wife hams it up
before presumably taking the snaps in
her jacket, formerly of the North Pole

168

Pleased to see them?

Alan Hudson manages to restrain his emotions – just about – in the company of models 'Renate' and 'Cindy'

TROUSERED

It takes a special type of character to show off some of these beauties – and that's not including the lovely 'Renate' and 'Cindy' opposite. Cockiness? Arrogance? Delusion? You be the judge...

It doesn't matter if it's black and white

Everton's Daniel Amokachi, with black MC Hammer-style trousers an added bonus

Diouf Class

After spitting at a Celtic supporter, Liverpool's El-Hadji Diouf (above left) perhaps thought the suit would suggest 'diminished responsibility' at Glasgow Sheriff Court in 2003

No material spared

Figure-hugging fare. Alan Hudson appears to be waiting for 'Renate' and 'Cindy' again

I score all those goals...

Roger Hunt's scored 245 league goals for Liverpool, but not in these pants. He needed to hunt for a new pair

Nott the best

Sol Campbell treads the London catwalk in these pyjama-style bottoms, proof that Notts County wasn't his worst move

Sporting casual

General manager Sir Stanley Matthews and his Port Vale trainer Len Graham (left in picture) attempt to get their message across – delivered in Olympic-issue fencing trousers

Maybe it was the vodka?

Graeme Sharp (below left) receives an award at Goodison Park in wool patchwork slacks

Pool bearers

Mo Johnston in swimming gear, Charlie Nicholas in all white. Both look silly

173

It's the fashion

George Best in figure-hugging maroon slacks with his then fiancée Eva Haraldsted outside his clothing boutique in Manchester's Bridge Street. Shouldn't he have worn something to try and persuade customers to go IN the shop?

Leathered

John Barnes outside the afterparty for film 'Maid In Manhattan' – yes, that's 'Maid In Manhattan'

Cisses about town

The introverted Djibril Cisse, in a jacket he may have borrowed off David Sullivan (page 93), and his wife Jude dress like anyone else would for a night out in Manchester

From both barrels

Ally McCoist and baggy Mo Johnston again. Do they have fashion in Scotland? **175**

Papa pants

Senegal striker Papa Waigo waves to fans after being introduced at Southampton's St Mary's Stadium. Hopefully they waved him towards the nearest shopping centre

Who are you then?

Don Revie shows where Steve McClaren got the idea from – the autograph hunter would seemingly prefer his own brolly

WATCH THE BIRDIE

A favourite pastime for people with time on their hands, it's no surprise footballers are keen players who like to look the part while ruining a good walk...

177

What happens when we go to the golf shop

England players fail to distinguish themselves for anything other than looking like they'd escaped from hospital at Royal Troon. Left to right: Gordon Milne, Gordon Banks, Bobby Moore, Maurice Norman, Roger Hunt

Medium size

In another life, he wore tasteful jumpers. Glenn Hoddle shows off his Pringle vintage, 1983

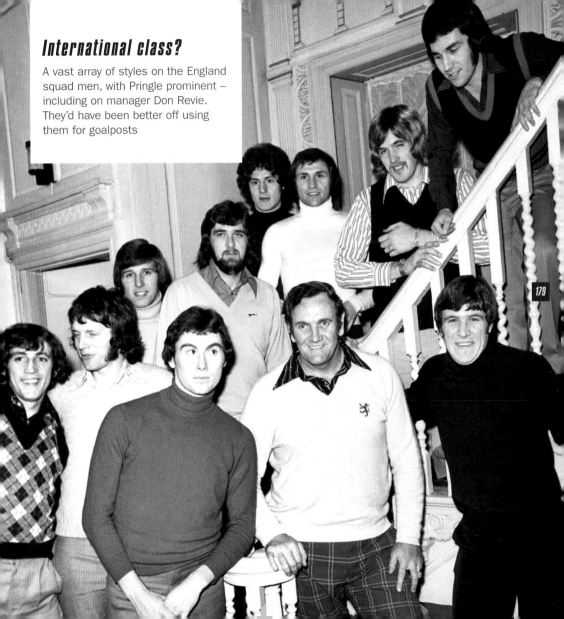

International class?

A vast array of styles on the England squad men, with Pringle prominent – including on manager Don Revie. They'd have been better off using them for goalposts

179

Kenny believe it

Dalglish and snooker legend
Stephen Hendry 'being Scottish'
at Gleneagles

Course designs

Kenny again, the then Blackburn Rovers
manager and – shock, horror! – Rangers
striker Ally McCoist. Is there nothing that
man will not wear?

Tea boy

Brian Kidd enjoys a cuppa after finishing
his round at Blackley Golf Club. For once,
the curtains look worse than a footballer's

Putting each other off

Big collars and cuffs, flowery shirts –
England players Emlyn Hughes and
Kevin Keegan at the fifth (above left),
May 1975. Left: The duo are joined
by David Johnson (centre) and all
could have kept their clubs up their
kecks

'Firey' centres

Everton midfield pair Paul Bracewell and Peter Reid witness the dangers of burping after a Mexican during a trip there in 1985

WE WEAR SHORT SHORTS

**The baggies of the 'olden days' were well
and truly put in the shade in the 1980s,
when footballers' shorts in particular were
adorned as though material rationing had
spread across the sporting landscape.
Such trends were maintained off the field too,
as these ball crunchers can testify...**

183

Tropical scene

Fabrizio Ravanelli models an 'outfit' as part of Dirk Bikkembergs' Spring-Summer 2007 men's collection (obviously). By 2008 we were all wearing the same (obviously)

Mirror man

West Ham's Julian Dicks agrees to have a Daily Mirror football kit painted on his naked torso during an April 1 promotion involving the newspaper and Pepsi. He looked Ridicksulous

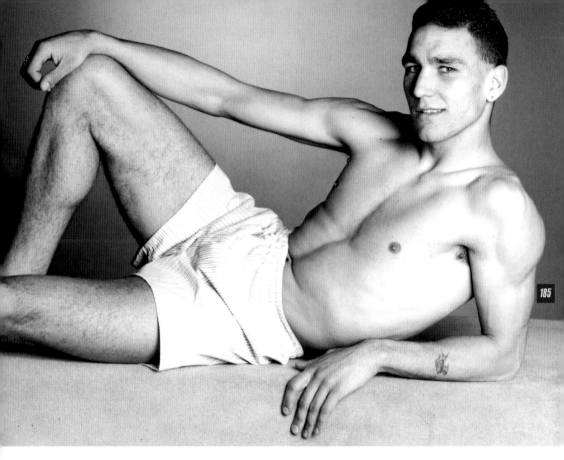

185

Boxer bad

Wimbledon's Vinnie Jones tries to make housewives go weak at the knees, which made a change from him kicking blokes below the knees, in a pair of baggy boxers

John Virgo special

Vinnie Jones, having now gone up in the world by joining Chelsea, models the latest in ill-advised suit addition – which even the snooker legend would have baulked at

WHAT A **WAIST(COAT)**

What a waste of money...

Italian style?

Roberto Baggio dons an
ill-fitting matching suit waistcoat

Sorry, 'olly

Ian Holloway brings out the waistcoat, which
on him was a waste of a coat

Fash in stripes

John Fashanu celebrates being cleared of all charges in a match-fixing trial by appearing to use pound coins as buttons on his waistcoat

Goals mean gaffs

Teddy Sheringham (over-sized waistcoat) and Ally McCoist (check jacket, colourful tie) receive their respective Golden Shoe awards in the 1992/93 season. Strangely enough, neither have ever won a British Fashion Award...

Pooling resources

Daniel Amokachi wouldn't be allowed in The Crucible Theatre in this open suede effort – and nor would his dog

Taking the Mick

Mick McCarthy clearly ran out of clothes at the 1990 World Cup finals in Italy so started wearing T-shirts that he'd bought for his family as souvenirs

WORLD CUP WILLIES

The greatest football show of them all deserves a section of its own. Sizzling summers, a trip abroad with the lads, the buzz of the team song and press photoshoots ... living in the tournament bubble can have disastrous consequences. Hard to believe some of these found their way into the designer suitcase...

Bloody Cowboys

Roy Aitken, Alex Ferguson and Graeme Souness must have mislaid the sombreros in Mexico '86 but luckily had packed their stetsons

Once upon a time in Mexico

Left: Can you spot which one of unlikely Scottish couple Graeme Souness and Alex Ferguson spent the most time topping up their tan?

Beret bad show

England players and backroom staff, including Trevor Brooking (left in picture), Glenn Hoddle (sixth left) and Peter Shilton (second right) don unnecessary Basque-style headware ahead of the 1982 World Cup fixture against Kuwait in Bilbao

Buy one, get one free

Summer hats, all the rage at the airport as the England squad relax with a 1970s-style iPod prior to World Cup finals in Mexico

Seeing the sights

England players including Emlyn Hughes (hat) and Brian Labone (third left) at the ancient Aztec pyramids before the tournament

Song for Deutschland

Scotland's 1974 squad in a London (yes, the capital of England) recording studio. Back row, left to right: George Connelly, Danny McGrain, Sandy Jardine, David Hay, Kenny Dalglish, Tom Forsyth.
Front, left to right: Erich Schaedler, Donald Ford, Willie Morgan, Ally Hunter, Jim Holton.
It's a fair guess that they bought the clothes north of the border...

New Order plus England 5

The England players who bothered to turn up for the recording of the 1990 collaboration with New Order which became 'World In Motion'. Back row, left to right: Chris Waddle (wing), Steve McMahon (midfield), John Barnes (rapper/wing), Peter Beardsley (forward), Des Walker (defence), Gillian Gilbert (keyboard), Stephen Morris (drums). Front row, left to right: Peter Hook (bass), Keith Allen (co-writer), Tony Wilson (Factory records part owner and manager)

Shining Example

Northern Ireland teenager Norman Whiteside's suit positively gleams as he returns from the 1982 World Cup a hero, and apparently with a birthday present for someone

Acceptable in the 80s?

Curtis Stigers was lost without his saxophone... Senegal coach Bruno Metsu (left), residing over his side's shock run to the quarter-final of the 2002 World Cup

Well, it was Chile

Pele wraps up to get his hands on the Jules Rimet trophy. If only he'd got his hands on a stylist

Lineker double

Gary Lineker 'relaxing' during the 1986 finals – Everton boss Howard Kendall sold him to Barcelona soon after and these pictures could well explain why

Oooh Betty!

It's Frank Spencer honing his opera voice, or maybe it's Geoff Hurst as part of the England squad singing 'Back Home' on *Top Of The Pops*, 1970. Back home, no-one was wearing dickie bows

Law unto himself

Striking legend Denis Law celebrates a free holiday to Argentina at the taxpayers' expense in London hours before leaving with the BBC team to cover the 1978 World Cup. In a kilt

Take the Rough with the smooth

He's got a skinny arm with no hand! No wonder he was shit in goal for Scotland... Goalkeeper Alan Rough's finest moment, after helping Partick Thistle to Scottish League Cup success

198

MISCELLANEOUS

**From Alf Inge Haaland's leather jacket and tie combo to Pat Nevin's black beret and brown overcoat, there have been a few fashion own goals that don't fit in any category.
Like an over-excited fan on the winning team's cup final picture, here are a few that have squeezed into our final cut...**

199

Cum On Feel The...

Life on Merseyside didn't seem all that bad for Liverpool's Peter Cormack. He apparently designed some of these clothes – whether the impressive leather and the Slade-style platforms form part of his fashion portfolio is uncertain, but his flares were amazingly wider than most Scouse gobs

Bad combination, young man

Nottingham Forest assistant manager Ronnie Fenton borrows one of Cloughie's green jumpers to welcome Norwegian signing Alf Inge Haaland – or is it Gordon Ramsay? – to the City Ground, 1993

Nevin again

When Pat Nevin auditioned for a presenter's role on Channel 4's *The Tube* he thought he'd be analysing the performances of Frankie Goes To Hollywood. Instead, he ended up on Channel 5 watching Fulham go to Hadjuk Bratislavawood

201

Out of the closet

Peter Reid (right) struggles in vain to find a shirt, trousers or a body that fits them

Bad Ron-jacket

Ron Atkinson (second right, above) rounds off his Saturday afternoon fever outfit with a medallion. Check out the flares on Alistair Brown (right). Mick Martin (above left) and Bryan Robson (above second left) are the other victims

The Kaizer chief

Hey DJ have you got Ninety Nein Red Balloons? A casual Franz Beckenbauer enjoys the US nightlife at the Xenon Disco with his 'companion' – despite the worst clash of his entire career

Doesn't suit you, senor

Argentina legends Diego Maradona and
Ossie Ardiles (above) arrive at Heathrow
Airport with a suitcase that is somehow
worse than their clobber. And to think
they got through nothing to declare!

Joleorange Lescott

Joleon Lescott, a beacon of style
for the MTV generation, goes for
the understated look – jeans
which look as though they've
been used for painting, and a top
as orange as most WAGs

203

204

Hello ladies...showing off the King's Road style

Fashionistas of the 1960s cited the King's Road as the place to be. Here's the proof that they were talking through their backsides, darling. Associated with icons such as Vivienne Westwood and Mary Quant, Chelsea, being the major football club in the area – sorry Fulham fans – enjoyed some fruits to this local link. Their star players, so legend goes, happened to enjoy the lively nightlife the area had to offer and would also indulge in the latest, ahem, 'fashions', sold by local boutiques. By April 1973 it is difficult to ascertain whether the designers had run out of ideas or were West Ham fans taking the piss. Make your own mind up by virtue of the evidence in this shot, involving Chelsea players and models. From left to right: Ian Hutchison, 'Cindy', Alan Hudson, 'Suze', Steve Kimber, 'Mynah Bird' and Bill Garner

Other Sport Media publications

In-depth analysis of a unique
relationship between the sides

A hilarious compilation of the
game's most bizarre injuries

Updated edition of the popular release
celebrating EFC games and moments

Unique look at Aston Villa's greatest
players from 1992 onwards

Other Sport Media publications

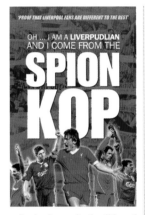

Revised paperback edition of Liverpudlians' Kop recollections

Stories and anecdotes from Chelsea's best footballers down the years

The top 10 Newcastle United best – as judged by journalist John Gibson

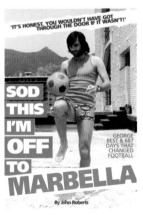

Fascinating portrait of the legendary Best between 1971-1973 (out July 2010)